Creating Books Covers with the GIMP for Self-publishing Beginners

Written by

Brian Jackson

I0492619

Version 3.0 – February 2021

Published by IIB Publishing

Discover other titles by Brian Jackson at
https://www.amazon.com/Brian-
Jackson/e/B003SRFYJY/ref=dp_byline_cont_pop_book_1

This book is dedicated to my wife and partner, my best friend, the person who sat by my side during its writing, the love of my life, Melanie.

Sign-up for My Mailing List

If you haven't already done so, be sure to sign up for my Amazon Kindle eBook Self-publishing for Beginners mailing list so that I can share new insights with you as I continue to hone my craft. Here's what you'll get:

- A free PDF copy of my book *Writer's Introduction to the Business of Self-publishing for Beginners*.
- Receive my weekly email newsletter.
- Receive updates on the *Amazon Kindle eBook Self-publishing for Beginners* series.
- Receive free and discount book offers.
- Receive free and discount Udemy online video training course offers.
- Receive plenty of new advice from the trenches as I continue to stumble upon new information and techniques.

I look forward to continuing to learn with you.

---Brian

1 Forward

What's the first thing you notice about a book, even an ebook, when shopping on Amazon, the world's largest retail bookseller? I'm willing to bet it's the cover. Even before you read the title or author name to see if you might be interested, it's typically the cover of the book that first catches your eye. That being the case, here's an important question I want you to ask yourself before we begin:

If my book cover is the most important element when it comes to getting my self-published book noticed and ultimately sold, then why am I not creating my book cover myself?

The answer to this question may very well be that there are no training materials available on how to create book covers. At least I haven't seen any. If this is what has been holding you back, I'd like to help by offering this manual to fill this significant vacuum in the pantheon of self-publishing literature.

I'm going to assume that you're already convinced that you want to at least try creating your own book cover; otherwise, why would you be reading this book? So, I won't spend a lot of time belaboring my case for doing it yourself. I will ask you to consider the following benefits to creating your own book cover:

1. It's fun.

2. It's easy.

3. It's fast.

4. It's inexpensive.

5. You get what you want.

Let's consider in more depth each of these benefits to doing it yourself.

Why in the world would you allow someone else to have the fun of creating your book cover for you? And then why would you pay them for it? Don't you realize the fun you're missing? (Sputter and grind teeth....)

You might be asking yourself how in the world creating quality book covers can be easy. The reason it's easy is that you have purchased this book that presents a methodology for making book covers that is simple yet powerful.

The methodology in this book involves selecting high-quality images off the Internet and combining them with colored boxes and text to produce book covers. That's it, no flashy stuff. In the end you are responsible for final assembly of the book cover, leaving the details of creating the images you use to the professional artists and photographers who post their art to the Internet from all over the world. This makes book cover creation easy.

Once you've mastered the basics of a graphics manipulation program such as GIMP, which is the program we'll be using in this manual, final assembly of a book cover is fast. This makes your artwork available on your schedule rather than someone else's.

Free fonts and color combined with one-dollar images produce book covers for well under five dollars apiece.

The bottom line is that you get exactly what you want, or at least what you're capable of creating, rather than depending on someone else's interpretation of your book cover vision.

At this point you should be asking yourself, so what is this manual I'm reading here? This manual is a step-by-step guide to using the GIMP image manipulation program to create book covers using inexpensive images downloaded from the Internet, free fonts, and colored boxes.

And what of the author? I've created hundreds of book covers for myself, my wife, and my author friends. To get a sense of the kinds of images I'll be teaching you to create in this manual, please browse my wife's website at the following URL:

http://www.melaniejackson.com

This guide was originally written as a set of text files that I planned to present as an online course over several weeks to a Romance Writers of America chapter on Long Island. Before the engagement folded on me I'd written the first five chapters of the presentation.

What was I to do?

I decided to convert my text files to HTML and post them to my blog, which garnered minor attention.

Well, that may not have been enough.

It turns out that there are a lot of people out there, mostly self-published authors, who want to know how to make book covers. Good book covers. I run into them all the time.

I'm writing this document in the interest of sharing what knowledge I've managed to accumulate regarding book cover design. Please join me on this voyage of discovery as we work together to sell your books.

2 Table of Contents

3 General Considerations

This section contains a few odds and ends, pointers on book cover design that I'd like to share before digging into the nuts and bolts of cover design. Consider them while working on your cover.

3.1 Keep Your Text Readable

Keep in mind that your book cover may look just fine to you in GIMP, based on the font style and text size selected, but shrunk to the size of an Amazon thumbnail portions of your graphics and text may begin to pixelate and fade into the background. You should always check to see what your cover looks like in thumbnail size using the View->Zoom->1:16 menu selection. Make sure that your primary text (e.g. the title and author name) is readable and that your images don't dissolve into general muck.

3.2 Visual Branding

Reuse fonts, color schemes, and images in a similar way on a set of book covers if they are related by genre, series, or author. This immediately tells your buyers that the books are a group and should be bought together.

For example, the Chloe Boston Mystery Series by my wife Melanie Jackson uses as its brand a specific font, a sloping hill, and a stack of illogical traffic signs on a post. Other images are included to represent season and plot, but the basic three elements of the brand remain the same from cover to cover.

Of course, branding can be extended into the title (e.g. "The Cat Who Wrote Murder Mysteries") and beyond to guide readers into reading related books written by the same author, you. Titles can also relate to the story through theme or repetition of word (e.g. *Dark Magic, Dark Revenge*, etc.). Also, inclusion of important keywords in your title can improve your odds of being noticed and purchased (keyword selection is a subject for another book).

For example, consider the following series of murder mystery covers and see if you can isolate what brands them together:

http://www.melaniejackson.com/chloe-boston-mystery-series

3.3 Keep It Simple

Don't try to summarize your book's entire plot on the cover. Choose one message or theme that best reflects your story and execute it well.

Keep cover text to a minimum. Title, author name, tag line, and optional bestseller designation (if you have it) are all you need. Anything else and you're probably overwhelming your reader.

Too many colors or garish color combinations can drive away potential customers. In fact, I've used nothing more than a single solid background color on some successful covers.

It's usually wise to content yourself with a single cover image.

3.4   Sample Book Covers

In support of this manual, I've setup an HTML page which displays a set of book covers that I created using the techniques outlined in this manual. Take a look at this page now by opening the following URL in your browser:

http://www.melaniejackson.com/brianjjaxn/bookCovers.html

We'll refer back to this page as we progress through the projects in this manual, but from now on we will refer to this page as The Wall of Book Covers.

4 Installing and Running GIMP

We'll begin by installing GIMP and beginning to use it. In this chapter, we will:

1. Learn a little bit about the GNU Image Manipulation Program (GIMP).

2. Install GIMP on your computer.

3. Learn to start and stop GIMP and review its major components.

4. Create a blank white image and save it.

5. Use the GIMP "Create" feature to create some cool web graphics and logos.

4.1 Overview of GIMP

The GNU Image Manipulation Program (GIMP) is an Adobe Photoshop–like graphics tool that allows you to manipulate images to produce, among other things, book covers. The program is very powerful and, best of all, it's free. We'll be using GIMP throughout this guide specifically to create book covers. As a result, we won't explore many of the tool's more powerful features. Instead, we'll stick to its basics, which are all you'll need to know to create quality book covers.

GIMP was developed and is maintained by the Free Software Foundation. You can visit the GIMP organization online at the following URL:

http://www.gimp.org

I encourage you to join the organization to defray some of their cost of operations.

4.2 GIMP Online Documentation

The GIMP User's Guide is the definitive reference for all things GIMP. The document is available online at the following URL:

http://docs.gimp.org/2.8/en/index.html

This document provides detailed usage information and examples for every feature of GIMP.

Go ahead and take a few moments now to familiarize yourself with the guide.

The GIMP User's Guide can also be accessed by clicking on the "Help" buttons located on the various GIMP screens. When accessing help through the GIMP program, a browser window will be opened displaying context-sensitive help for the specific GIMP screen on which help was requested.

In addition to the User's Guide, users have published many GIMP written and video tutorials on the Internet. Search for "gimp tutorial" in Google at the following URL:

> http://www.google.com

In addition to finding available tutorials you can enter "gimp" followed by a description of what you're trying to do.

4.3   Installing GIMP

It's time to install GIMP on your computer. Don't worry. With detailed instructions we'll try to make this as painless as possible.

4.3.1 Installing GIMP for Windows

If you're using a PC running the Windows operating system you should open the following URL in your web browser:

> http://www.gimp.org/downloads

A third of the way down the webpage is a link titled "Download GIMP 2.8". Left-click your mouse on this link.

In Windows 7, a small window will pop open at the bottom of the screen asking "Do you want to run or save gimp-2.8-i686-setup-1.exe?" In Windows XP a similar window will appear in the middle of the screen. Left-click your mouse on the "Run" button. Downloading will begin immediately and will take at least a couple of minutes to complete.

In Windows 7, you'll be asked "Do you want the following program to make changes to this computer?" If you see this message, click the "Yes" button. Alternately, your computer may say "A program needs your permission to continue." In which case you should select "Continue".

The GIMP installer "Welcome screen" will be displayed. Click the "Next >" button. The GNU "GNU General Public License" screen will be displayed. Again, click the "Next >" button. The "Ready to Install" screen will appear. Click the "Install now" button. . If instead you see a window with "Setup-GIMP" across the top, select "Install".

GIMP will now install itself. When it's done, the "Completing the GIMP Setup Wizard" screen will appear. Uncheck the "Launch GIMP" checkbox and click the "Finish" button.

The "GIMP 2" icon should now appear on your Windows desktop. Note that this icon will not appear if you've instructed Windows to not install icons on your desktop. In this case, access GIMP through the Start Menu.

4.3.2 Installing GIMP for MacOS

If you're a Mac user, open the following URL:

http://gimp.lisanet.de/Website/Download.html

Click on the appropriate version of the installation for your OS. The installation process should be similar to that for Windows described above with the following notes.

First, a few words about the Mac. I don't own a Mac and have rarely used one. This is the only Mac specific section in this guide. I'm hoping there aren't major differences between the Windows 7 version of GIMP that I describe in this guide and the version that runs on MacOS. If you get the chance, drop me a line at brianjjaxn@yahoo.com and let me know how your Mac experience differs. Thanks. Now, back to the installation....

The following is a note from author Susan Squires, who used these instructions to install GIMP on her Mac:

It works a little differently than your instructions for Windows, but most Mac users should be able to figure it out, if I can. When you click on the URL, it takes you to the SourceForge screen. You choose the version of Gimp that's right for your operating system, and that page even tells you how to look in your Apple menu, select About this Mac, to find out which version you have. I have Snow Leopard 10.6, and anything over 10.4 uses the latest version of GIMP. One caution might be that it doesn't have an indicator for Lion, which is the latest Mac Operating system. I have not downloaded Lion, because people say it takes some getting used to. But real Mac aficionados would have Lion already loaded. GIMP may work with Lion, but that isn't explicit.

When the program has finished loading, a window pops up with several icons in it. You move the dog picture into the App folder picture (there's an arrow there to illustrate what you're supposed to do.). That brings GIMP into your applications folder, where it is ready to open. Voila. I think it has fewer steps even than the directions you gave for Windows.

You might want to say that they need to wait for about 86 MB to download. If you try to work with the file before it's completely downloaded, you get some crazy messages.

4.4   Starting GIMP

To start GIMP, simply position your mouse pointer over the "GIMP 2" icon on your Windows desktop and double-click it with your left mouse button. GIMP will display a startup screen that shows you it's initialization progress. GIMP is ready to use when the Image Manipulation window appears.

Note: GIMP will be slow to start the first time as it gathers information about your particular installation.

Alternately, you can start GIMP from the Windows Start Menu by selecting All Programs->Gimp 2.

4.5   The GIMP Menu

The GIMP Menu provides access to all of the GIMP functionality. It runs across the top of the Image Manipulation window, beginning with "File" on the left and ending with "Help" on the right. To access a menu item, click and release your left mouse button while the mouse pointer is over the desired menu name, move your mouse down the menu, and left-click on the desired menu item.

Some menu items cascade. These items are displayed with a triangle to the right of the menu item name. To access a cascading menu, move your mouse pointer over the item and when the cascading menu pops up, move your mouse to the side to make your selection by left-clicking on a menu item.

To close a menu without selecting an item, simply left-click your mouse on the menu name or anywhere else outside the menu.

Note: This workshop will use the convention of identifying menu items by the menu (and optional cascading menu) on which they appear. For example, File->New refers to the "New" item on the "File" menu.

4.6 Displaying the Layers Window

Note that this step is only required if the Layers window is not already being displayed on your screen.

I display a standard window configuration while using GIMP which requires that you open the Layers window. To do this, select the Windows->Dockable Dialogs->Layers cascading menu item by clicking on the "Windows" menu and releasing your mouse button, moving your mouse down over the "Dockable Dialogs" item, moving your mouse to the side into the cascading menu to the "Layers" item, and clicking your left mouse button on the "Layers" item. When you perform this operation correctly, the Layers window will appear on your screen.

4.7 The GIMP Windows

Three windows should now be displayed by GIMP.

The Image Manipulation window (the one with the menu on top) is where the image being worked on is displayed. It currently displays a cartoon character because you're not working on an image. I like to position this window in the middle of my screen.

The Toolbox displays shortcuts to commonly used image manipulation tools on top, and configuration options for each tool on the bottom. I like to position this window on the left side of the screen.

The Layers window displays the layers of graphics that will be combined to produce the finished image. Use layers to work on discrete pieces of a complete image. We'll have more to say about layers in the Working with Layers and Selections chapter of this guide.

4.8 The File->New Menu Item

To create a new image, select the File->New menu item. This displays the "Create a New Image" dialog box. Book covers should be 1333 pixels in width by 2000 pixels in height. When creating a new book cover, enter these dimensions into the appropriate dialog box text fields and click the "OK" button to create the image.

4.9 The File->Save As and File->Save Menu Items

The File->Save As menu item allows you to save the image you're working on in a specific directory and file. This operation displays the "Save Image" dialog box. In the dialog box you can specify a directory to save your image in and a filename. I save all my images in the Windows 7 default "Pictures" directory.

You can name your book cover image file anything you want, but I like to name my files after the book they represent using reverse Polish notation. This involves removing the spaces and capitalizing all but the first word in the name. For example, the book cover for the book *Moving Violation* would be stored in a file named "movingViolation.xcf" in my "Pictures" directory.

Notice that the filename in the above example ends with the filename extension ".xcf". This signals to GIMP that the file should be saved in GIMP's native format so that it can be edited again later. Always save your work in progress in files concluding with the ".xcf" extension. Save your work in a file with the ".jpg" filename extension when you're ready to create a version of the image that you can use for publishing a book or on a website.

Once you've performed a File->Save As operation to establish the name and type of your file, you can use the File->Save menu item to save your latest work in the file you're currently working on.

Note: It's pretty easy to forget what the current file is and save all your latest changes in your ".jpg" files instead of your ".xcf" file. This can result in loss of work so look to the top window border on the Image Manipulation window to see what file you're currently saving to when using the File->Save operation.

4.10 The File->Open Menu Item

When you start GIMP to work on an existing project, use the File->Open menu item to open an image that you previously saved. Selecting this menu item will display the "Open Image" dialog box where you can select the image you want to work on by double-clicking your left mouse button on the image's filename.

Note that you can work with more than one image at a time by opening multiple image files in a single GIMP session. Each image will be displayed in a separate Image Manipulation window.

4.11 Closing Images and Quitting GIMP

Close an image without exiting GIMP by left-clicking with your mouse on the white "X" in the red box in the upper right corner of the Image Manipulation window containing the image. Alternately, you can use the File->Close menu item to perform the same operation. If you haven't saved the image displayed in the window, you will be prompted to do so. You then have the choice of saving or discarding your changes.

To close the GIMP application, left-click your mouse on the "X" in the upper right corner of the last remaining Image Manipulation window. Alternately, you can use the File->Quit menu item to perform the same operation. Again, you'll be prompted to save unsaved images if you have unsaved work in progress.

4.12 The Edit->Undo Menu Item

The most important operation in GIMP is accessed through the Edit->Undo menu item. The associated operation undoes the last modification that you made to an image. To experiment with GIMP, try an operation on an image. If you don't like the result, simply undo it. You can undo multiple operations by selecting Edit->Undo multiple times.

If you accidentally undo a modification you like, you can use the Edit->Redo menu item to reapply that modification. Additionally, there is an Undo History function which I find confusing so I stick to multiple executions of Edit->Undo to clean up after my mishaps.

Note that some operations, such a saving a file, cannot be undone.

4.13 Projects

4.13.1 Project 1: Install GIMP on Your Computer

Follow the instructions provided in the Installing GIMP section of this chapter to install GIMP on your computer.

4.13.2 Project 2: Create and Save a White Book Cover Image

Follow the instructions provided in this chapter to start GIMP, create a solid white 2000 x 1333 image, save the image in your "Pictures" directory as the name "bookCoversLesson1.xcf", and quit GIMP.

4.13.3 Project 3: Find a Book Cover to Emulate

Review the book covers I created at The Wall of Book Covers. See anything you'd like to use for your own cover? If not, browse Amazon or B&N looking for a cover you'd like to emulate.

4.13.4 Project 4: Simple Fun with GIMP

Experiment with the File->Create->Logos menu items to create interesting logos using various GIMP effects. Close each image created without saving the result and try the next effect. Once you've read this manual you'll be able to pull apart these compound images and use portions of them in your own work.

5   Creating a Simple Book Cover

In this chapter, we will:

1. Learn the three visual components of a book cover.

2. Learn how to save experimental images off the Internet onto our computer.

3. Bring an image into GIMP and resize it to exactly fit a book cover.

4. Change your view to fit the image in the Image Manipulation window.

5. Type text over the image and change the text style.

6. Save the resulting book cover.

5.1   Three Visual Components of a Book Cover

For the most part, book covers are composed of three major visual components.

One or more images are displayed in an attempt to tell the story of the book. The images are often colorful or provocative to draw attention.

Text is used to display the title, subtitle, series name, author's name, and a tag line or interesting selling point. The style of the text can also be used to tell something about the book's contents (e.g. a western style font versus a dripping blood font).

The third visual component is one or more colored boxes used to create geometric patterns or to set a contrasting color behind a font to make the print stand out better.

In this lesson, we'll focus on making a simple book cover by using a single image to cover the entire cover and placing stylized text over the top of the image. We'll address creating and placing colored boxes in a later chapter.

5.2   Saving Images from the Internet

When creating book covers, we must use images to which we hold the rights, so we'll be buying images from image vending sites or downloading them off government websites. In the meantime, when it comes to experimenting, we can use any image we find on the Internet.

The easiest way to find images to experiment with is to use your browser to open the Google search engine at http://www.google.com and click on the "Images" link in the top left of the screen to force Google to search for images. Enter a search keyword and click the "Google Search" button. Search strings such as "romance", "science fiction", and "nature" should produce interesting results.

Browse through the resulting images looking for an image that is book shaped (portrait), or could have a nice book-shaped chunk taken out of it, and that best tells the story of your book. When you find an image you like, click on it to display the largest available version. When the image is displayed, RIGHT-click on the image and select the "Save picture as..." menu item from the pop-up menu.

In the "Save Picture" window, save your picture in the "Pictures" directory using a descriptive filename such as "jungleWaterfall". Most pictures will automatically be saved as JPG formatted images.

Again, remember that such images may only be used for experimentation. When creating book covers, you want to use images to which you clearly own the rights.

5.3   Loading an Image into GIMP

The simplest way to load an image into GIMP is by opening it. Use the File->Open menu item to select the name of the file in the "Pictures" directory that you just saved. Double-click your left mouse button on the filename to open the associated image.

5.4   Scaling the Image

The next three steps introduce a standard method you should use when scaling an image to fill either an entire book cover, as in our case, or a rectangular region on a book cover.

Select the Image->Scale Image menu item. Within the "Scale Image" dialog box, type 1333 in the Width text box for the "Image Size" and press Enter. The image height will change to proportionally match the width of 1333. If the new image height is less than 2000, type an image height of 2000 and press Enter again. Click the "Scale" button at the bottom of the window to actually scale the image.

5.5 Zooming to Fit

As a result of increasing or decreasing the size of the image you're working on, you may want to zoom in or out on your work. Use the View->Zoom->Fit Image in Window menu item to best fit the image to the Image Manipulation window.

5.6 Cropping the Image

Note that if the width of your image is now 1333 and the height 2000 then you don't need to perform this step. Move on to the next step.

One dimension of your image now exactly fits the dimensions of a book cover while the other dimension is too long. Select the Image->Canvas Size menu item to crop off the unwanted height or width. Within the "Set Image Canvas Size" dialog box, click the chain symbol to the right of the Width and Height text fields to break proportionality. Type either 1333 over the incorrect width or 2000 over the incorrect height and press Enter. The dimension you did not type over should remain unchanged.

Click on the "Center" button on the middle right side of the dialog box. The picture below shows a white outline around the region of the image that will be retained after the crop is performed. To adjust the crop region, click your mouse in either the "X" or "Y" offset text fields (whichever is currently displaying a negative number) and use the up and down arrow keys on your keyboard to adjust the offset. Hold down the up or down arrow key to move the crop region faster.

When you have the white crop region around the portion of the image that you want to retain, click on the arrow to the right of the "Resize layers" option field and select "All Layers". Finally, click the "Resize" button at the bottom of the window to actually resize the image.

You now have a 2000 x 1333 book cover completely covered with an image. Follow this same procedure whenever filling a cover or region with an image to proportionally resize the image while cropping off as little of the image as possible.

5.7 Typing Text over the Image

To display text over your image, we'll use our first tool from the Toolbox window: the Text Tool. The Text Tool button looks like a large letter "A".

Left-click on this button in the top portion of the Toolbox window. The lower portion of the window changes to display options for configuring your text.

Note that you can move your mouse pointer over any tool buttons in the top half of the Toolbox window, without clicking the mouse, and a small tooltip will pop up to tell you what the button does.

Before placing your text, change the size of the text by entering "100" in the "Size" text box in the lower portion of the Toolbox window. Now, click anywhere on your image and type the title of your book, press Enter, and then type your name.

5.8 Moving the Text

Use the Move tool to move your text. Be sure to check the "Move the active layer" radio button in the tools options portion of the Toolbox window before using the tool.

To move your text, position your mouse pointer anywhere on the screen, click and hold down your left mouse button, and drag the text to where you want it. Release the left mouse button when you're done.

Text stands out the best when it isn't overlaying a complex portion of the image. For example, don't position the text over the faces of characters in an image. Also, text stands out best when light text is displayed over a dark portion of the image or dark text over light.

5.9 Changing the Text Content

To change the content of your text, simply position your cursor within the test in the Image Manipulation window and type your new text.

Note that sometimes when you add text to a selection, the text no longer fits properly within the text box. If this occurs, resize the text box by positioning your mouse pointer over the left or right side of the box until the cursor changes to an arrow pointed to a bar, hold down your left mouse button, and drag the text box outward to resize it.

After changing the text content, you should reposition the text box by repeating the previous step.

5.10 Changing the Text Size, Font, and Justification

Use the lower half of the Toolbox window to configure the selected text.

Use the "Size" text field to enter the font size for the text. Press Enter to cause your selection to take effect.

Click the "Aa" button to the left of the "Font" label to display a list of fonts to which you can change your text. The resulting pop-up selector displays a list of the fonts available on your computer with a small example of the font to the left (the letters "Aa" in the font). Scroll through the list and left-click your mouse on the font you'd like to use.

In a later lesson, you'll learn how to install additional free fonts from the Internet onto your computer.

To the right of the "Justify:" label are four options for justifying your text: left, right, centered, and filled. Click on one of these button options to select the justification you'd like. Remember that you can position your mouse pointer over these buttons without clicking your mouse to display a tooltip explaining what each button does.

You may need to stretch the text box to fit your text after changing the text's font or size.

Try to make your font as large as possible, but so the text still fits on the cover, to improve its readability. Also, select thick, bold fonts over spindly, willowy fonts so that the text remains readable when the book cover is displayed on the web as a thumbnail.

Select a font that reflects the content of your book. Pretty fonts are best for romance, blocky fonts for horror, and computer-looking fonts for science fiction.

5.11 Changing the Font Color

Click your left mouse button on the colored bar to the right of the "Color:" label to change the font's color. The "Text Color" dialog box will be displayed in response to your mouse click.

There are two common ways to select colors in the "Text Color" dialog box.

The first is to click your left mouse button on one of the predefined colors in the lower right corner of the dialog box. At first all these color boxes are blank. As you start trying different colors, your selections show up in the boxes.

The second is to mix your own color. To do this, left-click your mouse on the rainbow-colored vertical bar in the center of the screen to choose your color. Then, click and drag your mouse around the color box on the left of the screen to select the brightness of the color. Note that the color displayed to the right of the "Current:" label will change to show your current color.

Click the "OK" button in the lower right of the dialog box to set your text color or "Cancel" to dismiss the dialog box without changing the text color.

Text stands out the best when you use dark-colored text over a light image or light-colored text over a dark image. As a result, white and black are the two most popular text colors for book covers because they stand out the best.

Avoid garish colors such as bright yellow. Set the text color to reflect the type of book: red is good for horror while pastels are best for romance.

5.12 Zooming Out to View a Thumbnail of Your Cover

To see if your text remains readable when your book cover is displayed on a website as a thumbnail, use the View->Zoom menu item to zoom out to an aspect ratio of "1:16". If you can still read your title in this thumbnail view, your book cover should look good when you load it on Amazon and other online book vendor sites.

Reset your view when you're done by selecting the View->Zoom->Fit Image in Window menu item.

5.13 Saving the Result in XCF and JPG Formats

When saving our work, there are two file formats we need to consider: XCF and JPG. XCF is the native GIMP file format. When you save a file in XCF format, you save all the information about the GIMP image. Use this information for work in progress. JPG is the image format you'll use to display an image on the web or to submit it for publication. When you save a file in JPG format, you save only a raster image. While working on an image, save it in XCF format. When you want to cut a snapshot to view outside GIMP, save a JPG formatted image.

When you're reasonably happy with your book cover (don't worry, our covers will get better), first save it as a JPG image using the File->Export menu item. Save your work in the "Pictures" directory and name it using reverse Polish notation with the ".jpg" file extension (e.g. theSecretStaircase.jpg). GIMP will display the "Export File" dialog box. Click "Export".

Now use the File->Save As menu item to save the image in XCF format by following the same process as above but using the ".xcf" filename extension (e.g. theSecretStaircase.xcf). Notice that in this instance you won't be prompted with the dialog boxes.

5.14 Learning from Existing Book Covers

The best way to learn what constitutes a cool book cover is to browse Amazon or some other online bookseller for cool book covers. As you do so, make note of the elements of the covers that you'd like to use on your own cover. By the time you finish this workshop, you should possess the knowledge required to replicate most book covers.

5.15 Projects

5.15.1 Project 1: Review the Book of Dreams Covers

The book covers that I created for Melanie and my Book of Dreams Series are basically text over full cover image covers. Check out the following website to see how effective this simple technique can be:

http://www.melaniejackson.com/V2/BoD.shtml

Click on each book cover to display a larger image.

Notice that I used different-sized fonts for different text elements (you'll learn how to do this in the next lesson) and made the mistake of using a willowy font for some of the writing (it doesn't show up well in thumbnail).

5.15.2 Project 2: Create Your First Book Cover

Follow the instructions in this lesson to create and save your own simple book cover in both XCF and JPG formats.

6 Working with Layers and Selections

In the lesson, we will learn:

1. About layers and the Layers window.

2. How to manipulate layers.

3. How to select text and graphic regions.

4. How to copy and cut text and graphics.

6.1 Using the Layers Window

Layers are the fundamental building blocks of an image. They allow you to work on individual components of an image while leaving the rest of the image alone. When stacked on top of one another, layers are combined to produce a finished image. The contents of layers higher in the stack block out the contents of layers beneath them. As a result, transparent layers containing text and graphics are the most popular layers to stack. Typically, the lowest layer contains a solid color or background image that covers the entire book cover.

The Layers window shows you the layers that have been defined in an image and the order in which they're stacked. You can use commands in the Layers window and the buttons at the bottom of the window to manipulate the layers.

Use the File->Open menu item to open the book cover you saved in the previous lesson. It should contain two layers: one layer named "Background" which contains the image and a text layer containing the title of the book and your author name. The name of the text layer will be the text it contains. Since the text layer is above the image layer, its contents block out the contents of the image directly below the text (the area of the text layer other than the text is transparent).

By the way, transparency is displayed in GIMP as a checkerboard of light and dark gray squares.

When adding a new graphic or text component to a book cover, create it on a new layer so that you can individually manipulate and position it.

6.2   Selecting a Layer

To work with a layer, you must first select it in the Layers window. The selected layer is displayed as light gray in the window. To select a layer, click on its name. The operation you perform in the Image Manipulation window will then affect only the contents of the selected layer.

Note that the number one reason that things go wrong when working with GIMP is that you don't have the correct layer selected when working on an image. If you want to modify the text of your book cover, first click on the text layer in the Layers window. If you try to select the text box while the image layer is selected, nothing will happen. If you want to work on the image, first click on the "Background" layer.

6.3   Adding and Duplicating a Layer

To add a layer above the current layer, click on the button in the lower left corner of the Layers window (it looks like a piece of paper with the top right corner folded down). Remember, by placing your mouse pointer above a button without clicking it a tooltip will appear explaining the purpose of the button.

The "Create a New Layer" dialog box will be displayed. In this dialog box you can name the new layer and choose whether it should be filled with the foreground color ("Black"), the background color ("White"), White, or it should be transparent. In most cases you will want a transparent layer so that only the things you place on the layer will block the contents of lower layers. Click the "OK" button to create the layer.

Use the "Duplicate Layer" button, the fourth button over at the bottom of the Layers window, to duplicate the current layer.

6.4   Raising and Lowering a Layer

Because the contents of higher layers block the contents of lower layers, layer order is important. Use the up and down arrows at the bottom of the Layers window to move the current layer up and down through the layer stack.

6.5   Making a Layer Invisible and Visible

Click the garbage can in the lower right corner of the Layers window to delete the current layer. Note that you can use Edit->Undo to undo this operation.

6.6   Deleting a Layer

Click the garbage can in the lower right corner of the Layers window to delete the current layer. Note that you can use Edit->Undo to undo this operation.

6.7   Merging Two Layers

Sometimes it's useful to deal with the contents of two layers as a single element. In this case, the layers should be merged.

First, use the up and down arrows to insure that the two layers to be merged are next to each other. Right-click on the layer on top and select "Merge Down" from the pop-up menu. The two layers will be merged to produce a single layer.

6.8   Image, Text, and Floating Layers

As you work with GIMP, you'll come across three types of layers that display themselves differently in the Layers window.

Image layers are layers that contain graphic elements. They display themselves in the Layers window as a thumbnail of the image contents in the box to the left of the layer name.

Text layers are layers that contain text that can be modified using the Text Tool. They display themselves with the letter "A" in the box to the left of the layer name.

Floating layers are selections that have not yet been anchored onto a layer. These appear in the middle of a Cut & Paste or Copy & Paste operation. Be sure to anchor your layers before performing further work by clicking on the anchor symbol at the bottom of the Layers window.

6.9 Layer Opacity

Use the Opacity slider in the Layers window to make a layer ghostly,
allowing lower layers to bleed through. Play with this effect on your own by
moving the slider back and forth to understand its use.

It can quite often help to put a black or white background behind a partially
opaque layer to allow the darkness or lightness to bleach an image in the
current layer.

6.10 Selecting All and None

In the remainder of this lesson, we'll learn how to select all or a portion of a
layer for Cut & Paste or Copy & Paste operations. In a later lesson, we'll use
selection with the Bucket Tool to create colored boxes.

Before selecting anything, ensure that the correct layer is selected in the
Layers window.

To select everything on a layer, use the Select->All menu item. A border,
known as marching ants, will surround your selection.

To turn off a selection (when no longer needed), use the Select->None menu
item.

6.11 Using Rectangular Selection

To select a rectangular portion of a layer, use the Rectangle Select Tool
located in the upper left corner of the Toolbox window. After selecting this
tool, your mouse cursor will turn to a "+" in the Image Manipulation
window. To use it, position the plus sign to the upper left of the selection,
hold down your left mouse button, and drag your mouse to the lower right
corner of the selection. A green/purple box will be used to show your
selection.

When you release your left mouse button, marching ants will be used to
show the boundaries of your selection. You can move your mouse pointer
over any side or corner of the selection and click and drag your mouse to
increase or decrease the size of the selection. You can click and drag in the
center of the selection to move it.

6.12 Using Elliptical Selection

Similar to the rectangular selection tool but creates an elliptical selection. The button to enable this tool is directly to the right of the Rectangle Selection Tool. Use it to produce circular selections.

6.13 Using Free Selection

The Free Select Tool, the lasso to the right of the Ellipse Select Tool, can be used in two ways to perform free-form selection.

First, you can hold your left mouse button down while dragging the mouse pointer around the Image Manipulation window to create your selection. Second, you can repeatedly click your left mouse button to create a series of straight lines to form your selection. You can alternately use both methods to create your selection. To close your selection, move your mouse to the start point of the selection while holding your mouse button down or click over your start point.

Use free selection to select complex shapes. In a later lesson, we'll learn to use the erase tool to clean up our selection.

6.14 Using Color Selection

Color selection allows you to select everything on the layer of a particular color. To use it, select the tool (second from the right on the top row) and click on a color. Marching ants will appear around all occurrences of that color on the layer.

Note that you can drag the "Threshold:" slider to the right to select colors that are farther and farther from being close to the color you select. A better way to add close colors to the selection is outlined in the following section.

6.15 Adding and Subtracting Selection

You can use any of the above selection methods to add to an existing selection by holding down the Shift key on your keyboard before performing the selection. You can remove portions of a selection by holding down the Ctrl key and doing the same.

The addition selection technique is most useful when performing color selection. In this case, choose the color selection tool, hold down the Shift key, and continue to add colors to your selection by clicking on colored pixels in the Image Manipulation window. If you accidentally select a color you don't want, use the Edit->Undo menu item to remove the selection.

If color selection results in selecting a portion of the image you didn't want to select (e.g. you're selecting a flower and some words get selected), you can hold down the Ctrl key and select the portions of the selection you want to remove from the current selection (e.g. using rectangular selection).

Using selection addition and subtraction, you can use all of the techniques outlined in this section to build a complex selection through several operations.

6.16 Inverting Your Selection

Sometimes it's easier to select what you don't want than it is to select what you do want. In these cases, select what you don't want and invert your selection. For example, if you want to select a complex image on a solid white background, it's easy to select the solid white background with one Select by Color Tool click and invert the selection to select everything not currently selected.

Use the Select->Invert menu item to unselect everything selected and select everything not selected. Note that you can use inversion in the middle of building a complex selection using multiple selection and deselection steps.

6.17 Moving a Layer

Since we'll be following the convention of placing a single graphical element on separate transparent layers, we can move graphical elements around our book cover by moving the layer. Use the Move Tool to move a graphical element.

To use this tool, select the correct layer, click and hold down your left mouse button over the graphical element, and drag it to its new location. Release your mouse button when you're done.

Don't worry if the outline of your layer overlaps the borders of your image, it will be cropped to fit.

6.18 Copy & Paste

Once you've selected a portion of an image, you can make a copy of it by selecting the Edit->Copy menu item, moving to a new layer by adding a layer or selecting a layer in the Layers window, and using Edit->Paste to paste the selection into the new layer.

6.19 Cut & Paste

Cut & Paste is like Copy & Paste above, except that you remove the selected region from the source layer and paste it to its destination. Use this technique to move an image or colored box around the image.

6.20 Copying from One Image to Another

Note that you can select and copy a region of an image or text from one image to another by opening the image you want to copy from using File->Open, creating your selection in the opened Image Manipulation window, executing Edit->Copy from that window, then selecting a different Image Manipulation window in which to perform you Edit->Paste.

When you select one of multiple open Image Manipulation windows by clicking your left mouse button somewhere in the window, or on its border, the Layers window changes to show you the layers in the selected Image Manipulation window. Working with multiple images at a time is key to creating a complex book cover.

Use this technique to copy images from multiple sources onto a single book cover. Remember to always paste to a new transparent layer.

6.21 Projects

6.21.1 Project 1: Modify Your First Book Cover

Modify your first book cover by removing the author name following the book title and reentering each as separate text layers.

To add a new text layer, simply select the Text Tool ("A") in the Toolbox window and click somewhere on your image outside an existing text box. Being sure to select the correct layer for modification, change your author name to a smaller font. Now move the title and the author name separately, after changing to the appropriate layers, to place them in the best locations on your cover.

Pay particular attention to the contents of Saving Images from the Internet through Cropping the Image in Chapter 3.

7 Loading Fonts and Using Text Effects

In this chapter, we will:

1. Learn about selecting fonts and using multiple text layers.

2. Learn to align and center text.

3. Load new fonts off the Internet.

4. Manipulate fonts with effects.

5. View book covers as thumbnails.

7.1 Choosing Fonts

When choosing fonts for your cover, you should opt for thick fonts that will show up well when the cover is displayed as a thumbnail image. Yes, those willowy fonts are pretty, but their thin lines tend to disappear when the cover is displayed as a small image. So, go with the more substantial fonts.

Choose a font style that matches the style of your book. Whether the font is pretty, grungy, cartoony, or professional should be determined by whether the book is pretty, grungy, cartoony, or professional. Use your fonts to tell your story.

Times New Roman in plain and italic is a good choice for subtitles and "New York Times Bestseller" above your author name (should you be so lucky).

7.2 Fonts and Branding

We haven't discussed branding yet, but this is an important issue. Branding involves using common graphic elements on all your book covers to unite them. Whether uniting all the books in a series or all your books, using common fonts on each book cover can help to establish your brand.

For example, you may want to use the same font for the titles of all your books in a series and share the same author name style and location on every book. It's easy to copy common elements from one book cover image to another or use an existing cover as a template for the next book.

7.3   Using Multiple Text Layers

Each time you add text to an image it produces a new text layer. Each text layer can use a different font, different size, and different color. Additionally, each text layer can be moved around the image independently.

I often use different text layers for each line of text when producing multiline text elements (e.g. titles). Rather than accept the interline spacing forced upon me by including a new line in a text block, I position each line myself (often to crowd the lines together).

You may also want to use the technique of displaying a text element all in uppercase but making the first letter of each word, or the first word, larger. To do this, enter two separate text layers, the first with a larger font then the rest of the letters. Align the two layers to produce a word and merge the layers together to form a single word when you're done manipulating the font information for the text layers.

7.4   Aligning Text

To align multiple text layers along a horizontal plane, I simply zoom in on the text to be aligned (e.g. 2:1) and manually align it. There are more sophisticated ways of doing this, but my way is quick and simple.

To zoom in on your text, select View->Zoom->2:1. Scroll the Image Manipulation window horizontally and vertically until the text you're trying to align is displayed and move the text to align it. Select View->Zoom->Fit Image in Window when you're done to display the entire image in the Image Manipulation window.

I use the same method to align text along a vertical plane.

7.5   Centering Text

The easiest way to center text on a cover is to:

Select the text box to be centered by selecting the Text tool, selecting the correct layer, and clicking on the text.

Stretch the text box so that the left and right edges of the box are aligned with the left and right edges of the cover.

Select "Centered" from the "Justify:" options in the configuration section of the Toolbox.

7.6   Loading Free Fonts off the Internet

GIMP uses the fonts that are loaded on your computer. You can augment your existing font library by loading free fonts off the Internet.

My favorite free font download site is:

>   http://www.dafont.com

Go to this site and browse the font list. When you find a font you like, click the "Download" button. When prompted by your operating system, select "Open". You'll be presented with an open zip file. Double-click on the TrueType font within the file and "Open" it. Click the "Install" button at the top of the window to install the font.

Note that you'll have to restart GIMP to gain access to newly loaded fonts.

Avoid selecting fonts that are labeled "Free for personal use".

7.7   Text vs. Image Layers

Text layers retain all the information related to the text they contain including the font, size, and color. Some text manipulation operations convert a text layer to a graphic layer and this information is lost. Be sure you've set your font, size, and color before performing any of the following manipulations since they will turn your text into a graphic.

Note that merging multiple text layers will also produce a merged graphic layer.

7.8   Scaling Text

Use the Scaling Tool to stretch text either vertically or horizontally. I often use this method to stretch my big fat fonts vertically to make them taller.

To use this technique, select the Scaling Tool in the Toolbox. Select the text layer to stretch then select the text box to stretch. Boxes will appear on all sides and corners of the text box. Grab a side and start pulling. When done, select the "Scale" button in the "Scale" dialog box. Select the "Cancel" button to reject your changes.

7.9   Rotating Text

Use the Rotate Tool to rotate text off the horizontal plane.

41

To use this technique, select the Rotate Tool in the Toolbox. Select the text layer to stretch then grab a side of the box and move it up or down, left or right. When done, select the "Rotate" button in the "Rotate" dialog box. Select the "Cancel" button to reject your changes.

7.10 Shearing Text

Use the Shear Tool to cant text to the left or right.

To use this technique, select the Shear Tool in the Toolbox. Select the text layer to shear then grab a side of the box and move it left or right. When done, select the "Shear" button in the "Shear" dialog box. Select the "Cancel" button to reject your changes.

7.11 Adding Perspective to Text

Use the Perspective Tool to make it look like your text is disappearing into the distance.

To use this technique, select the Perspective Tool in the Toolbox. Select the text layer to change then grab the right top side of the box and pull it down. When done, select the "Transform" button in the "Perspective" dialog box. Select the "Cancel" button to reject your changes.

Note that you can use this technique in combination with shearing and rotation to make text look like it's racing into the distance.

7.12 Blurring Text and Creating Drop Shadows

You can add a simple blur to text using Filters->Blur->Gaussian Blur. Experiment to see what this does.

A commonly used blur effect is a drop shadow. It's so commonly used that GIMP now offers it as a single step function (you used to have to do it yourself). Select Filters->Light and Shadow->Drop Shadow to produce a blurred black shadow just below the text. This effect helps to make light text stand out against a light background.

7.13 Applying Filters to Text

You can apply a ton of effects to text. I find it easiest to use most of these effects via the File->Create->Logos menu option that you experimented with in Simple Fun with GIMP. To use any of the text effects created, delete the background layer (we want the background to be transparent) then merge all layers and layer masks until you have a single layer. You can then copy this text effect to your book cover image as a new layer.

7.14 Viewing Book Covers as Thumbnails

Periodically, you should view your cover image as a thumbnail to insure that your text is readable in small versions of the image. To do this, select View->Zoom->1:16. Is your text still readable? When done viewing the thumbnail, select View->Zoom->Fit Image in Window to fill the Image Manipulation window with your image.

7.15 Projects

7.15.1 Project 1: Load a Free Font

Visit http://www.dafont.com and load a new font onto your computer.

7.15.2 Project 2: Try the Text Effect Tools

Experiment with the Scale, Rotate, Shear, and Perspective Tools to manipulate text layers. Add a drop shadow. Play with the drop shadow parameters to see what they do. Experiment with other Filter effects as time and interest permit.

7.15.3 Project 3: Update Your Simple Cover

Refer to *He's a Magic Man* at The Wall of Book Covers in your web browser:

Notice how I used multiple fonts and font sizes to build the text on this cover. I used 12 text layers to produce the text. Notice the different font used to highlight the letter "M" in Magic and Man.

7.15.4 Project 4: Update Your Simple Cover

Use the techniques you've learned in this chapter on your simple book cover to add multiple text layers and text effects as desired.

8   Buying and Manipulating Inexpensive Images

In this chapter, we will:

1. Buy inexpensive professional images off the Internet.

2. Position and manipulate images on a book cover.

8.1   Getting Free Images From Pixabay

This is an update to this document. In recent years, I've obtained all of my images off of a free site named Pixabay (https://www.pixabay.com). The remaining information on free and inexpensive images is still helpful, but I find that Pixabay satisfies all of my image needs.

Pixabay images are free for virtually any use including commercial use (just don't resell the images unmodified).

8.2   Free Image Sites: Do You Trust Them?

There are plenty of free images in the public domain on the Internet. I don't use them for several reasons. The primary reason is that I feel like unless I'm paying a specific person to grant me the rights to their work that I'm in danger of accidentally using a work without the artist's permission. I'd rather pay the artist a buck or two per image and know that I'm getting the rights to the piece directly from the acknowledged artist.

For those who would like to save a few bucks, here is an email extract from Lisa Cach, an author friend who has become an accomplished cover artist herself.

Here's a long list of public domain sources at Wikipedia:

> *http://en.wikipedia.org/wiki/Wikipedia:Public_domain_image_resou rces*

My go-to places are:

The Yorck Project (horribly organized)

> *http://commons.wikimedia.org/wiki/Category:PD-Art_(Yorck_Project)*

WikiPaintings (unrelated to Wikipedia)

http://www.wikipaintings.org

I'd add, about WikiPaintings, that not all art on the site is public domain, but they tell you which is which; and you can sometimes find higher resolution versions of the same images elsewhere online. But I like the site because you can search on subject matter, like "ghost" or "kiss".

8.3   Buying Images off the Internet

Inexpensive professional images can be purchased of the Internet for very little money. When you purchase these images, you are actually purchasing the rights to use them on your book covers. My favorite site to purchase book cover images is http://www.canstockphoto.com. Go ahead and open the website in your browser and take a look around.

To find images, enter your search criteria at the top of the screen (e.g. "romantic vampire") and click the "Search" button. The screen will be filled with thumbnails of images matching your selection. To see a larger version of an image, simply move your mouse pointer over an image or click on the image to display its purchase screen. To constrain your search, check the box next to "Photos" to display only photos.

Typically, you'll be looking for cover-shaped, portrait-sized images unless your image is to be displayed in a stripe across the cover. Purchase an appropriately sized image. In most cases you can get away with resizing the lowest resolution images but for full cover shots you may want to choose a larger image.

To purchase images off Can Stock Photo, you'll need to create an account and purchase credits. Credits are bought in bundles of from 15 to 450 for as little as $0.44 a credit. The images you purchase will most often cost no more than 2 to 4 credits. I'd recommend buying only 15 credits at first since you don't save all that much on volume purchases.

There are other sites where you can purchase inexpensive professional images including http://www.istockphoto.com.

As mentioned earlier, don't just randomly use images off the Internet on your book covers since you won't own the rights.

Another alternative for obtaining images is to go to a government site such as http://www.usa.gov/Topics/Graphics.shtml where your taxes pay for the right to use certain images.

8.4   Purchasing an Image on Can Stock Photo

The following list outlines step by step how to purchase an image off Can Stock Photo once you've paid for your credits.

1. Enter your search criteria and click the Search button to display a list of potential images.

2. Choose an image by double-clicking on it to display its purchase page.

3. Select the appropriate size, check the "'I accept" box, and click the Download button.

4. The "Do you want to download…" box will appear at the bottom of the screen.

5. Use the Save As option to save your image in a known directory.

8.5   Downloading Comps off the Internet

Most sites that allow you to purchase image rights also allow you to download a "comp", or complimentary copy of the image. The comp will be low resolution and have ghostly writing over the top of it but you can use it to mock up your cover before committing to purchasing your cover art. I recommend that you always create a proof or concept copy of your cover before buying the art work.

On the Can Stock Photo image purchase webpage, there is a hyperlink below the image named "Save Comp". Once selected, downloading the image works the same as with purchased images. Note that you may want to create a separate folder for comps so as not to confuse them with the real images.

8.6   Using Images

If the image you purchase is to be used as the background for your cover, use the method outlined in Creating a Simple Book Cover (Chapter 3) to size it. Then you can use the image as the base for your cover or copy the image (Select->All followed by Edit->Copy) to your cover image replacing the background (the lowest layer).

If the image you purchased is to be used on a portion of your cover (e.g. a strip across the middle), use the method outlined in Creating a Simple Book Cover to size and crop the image as needed. For example, to do a stripe across the cover, use Image->Scale Image to proportionally set the width to 1333, the use Image->Canvas to crop the image to a height of the desired size (e.g. 300). Be sure to click the chain symbol before setting your Image->Canvas to break proportionality when cropping. When you're done, Select->All and Edit->Copy the image and Edit->Paste it to a new layer on your book cover.

After manipulating a purchased image, be sure to save the result in a new file or discard it after copying so that you can retain an original of the purchased image.

8.7   Flipping Images

To flip an image horizontally, select the Flip Tool and then select the correct layer and click on the image. The image will flip left to right. Note that you can flip text as well (though I don't know why) which will turn it into a graphic layer. You can also flip vertically (upside down) by clicking the Vertical button in the lower pane of the Toolbox window.

I often flip an image to more easily place it on a side of a cover away from the location in which I intend to place text. It also makes for nice reflections as on the *Of Two Hearts* cover on The Wall of Book Covers webpage.

8.8   Rotating Images

Use the Rotate Tool to rotate an image in the same way that you would use the tool to rotate text. I use this technique to produce the effect of photographs scattered on a table top or to fit an irregularly shaped image into a blank spot on a cover.

To use the tool, simply grab a corner of the image and spin it. The Rotate window will appear to display the angle at which you're rotating the image. Alternately you can produce an exact rotation (e.g. 90 degrees) by typing a value in the "Angle" field of the Rotate window.

8.9   Cropping Images

The Crop Tool provides a handy and quick way to resize an image. It's like the Rectangle Select Tool except that the area you're selecting represents what you'd like left after cropping the image. Also like the Rectangle Select Tool you can type "Position" and "Size" information in the bottom half of the Toolbox window to perform precise cropping to a specific size.

Note that you can alternately use the Images->Canvas Size menu selection to perform image cropping.

8.10 Zooming and Panning

You can use the View->Zoom->2:1 menu selection to zoom in on your image in order to perform precise alignment. For example, zooming in can be useful when creating drop shadows or marrying two images.

Once you've zoomed in on the image you can use the horizontal and vertical scroll bars to pan around the image.

When you're done with your detail work, use the View->Zoom->Fit Image in Window menu selection to return the image to its optimal viewing size.

8.11 Cutting Out Images

You'll occasionally find the need to extract portions of a photograph that can't be selected by using color selection or through the use of rectangular or elliptical regions. Examples include extracting a person, building, or tree from a background. In these cases you should use the Free Select Tool to outline portion of the image to be selected.

Before outlining, be sure to zoom in on the image using the View->Zoom menu selection. Zoom back out when you're done using View->Zoom->Fit Image in Window.

Click the Free Select Tool in the Toolbox window. Begin your selection by left-clicking your left mouse button over the edge of the outline you'd like to produce. You're presented with a point attached to a string. Move your mouse pointer to the next location along the outline and click again. Continue to outline the desired shape in this way until you have closed the select by clicking on your original point.

Once the selection is closed, the points and lines of your selection will be replaced by the marching ants that indicate a completed selection. Once this happens you can copy or delete your selection.

8.12 Using Layer Opacity

Reducing a layer's opacity makes that layer more transparent, allowing the contents of lower layers to show through from beneath. To adjust a layer's opacity, select the layer to be affected in the Layers window then slide the

Opacity bar at the top of the Layers window left or right to apply less or more opacity.

Layer opacity is great for creating ghostly overlays and taking down the intensity of an image.

You may want to place a white or black background behind the layer on which you'll be changing opacity to let either light or dark bleed into the image from below.

8.13 Projects

8.13.1 Project 1: Buy an Image and Scale It to Cover Size

Go to canstockphotos.com or some other suitable site and purchase and download an image. Make note of where you save it, open it, and set it to the full size of a book cover (2000 x 1333 pixels).

9 Creating Colored Boxes

Let's talk about how to add a splash of color to your book cover with limited effort. Besides that, colored banners and boxes can be useful in setting text off from images and setting images off from the background color.

In this chapter we will discuss:

1. How to create a rectangular selection and fill it with color.

9.1 Creating a Layer per Colored Box

Go to the Layers window and click on the New Layer icon at the bottom left corner of the window. This will create a new layer in which to place your colored box. Be sure that this layer is in the correct location in the layer hierarchy to overlay background and fall before foreground images.

Be sure to store one graphical element per layer to allow easy manipulation of your overall image.

9.2 Selecting a Rectangular Region

Click on the Rectangle Select Tool in the upper left corner of the Toolbox window. Then go to the Image Manipulation window and drag your mouse over the area you'd like to fill with color.

Note that after you've created a rectangular selection, the location at which your selection begins and its size will be displayed in the bottom half of the Toolbox window. You can type new Position coordinates and Size parameters over these values to fine tune your selection.

For example, you might want to create a 300-pixel-high colored band spanning the center of your book cover. Such a band should be 1333 pixels wide and begin at offset 0 from the left border and be 300 pixels high beginning at an offset of 850 pixels. This kind of minor math and precision selection makes for quality book covers.

9.3 Selecting Foreground Colors

Next you should pick the color that will be used to fill your rectangular selection. At the bottom of the tools section of the Toolbox is the foreground selection box (about a third of the way down the screen). The foreground color selection box is in front of the background selection box.

Double-click your left mouse button on the foreground color selection box. A fairly standard color selection dialog box will be displayed. Here you can select your fill color.

9.4 Using the Bucket Fill Tool

Click your left mouse button on the Bucket Fill Tool in the Toolbox window. Ensure the "Fill whole selection" radio button is selected. Click within the rectangular selection to dump your foreground color into the box.

9.5 Sampling Colors

Sometimes you may want to fill a rectangular selection with a color from an accompanying image or color you used on another cover. To do so, select the Color Picker Tool from the Toolbox window (it looks like an eyedropper).

Go to the Image Manipulation window associated with the image from which you'd like to select a color. Ensure that you have the proper layer selected in the Layers window. Finally, click on the color you'd like to sample.

After clicking on the desired color, the foreground color displayed in the center of the Toolbox window will change to reflect the newly sampled foreground color. Continue to sample colors until you get the color you want.

Once the desired color has been selected, use the Bucket Fill Tool to fill a rectangular region with the color.

9.6 Capturing Screen Shots

So, what do you do if you want to sample a color off a webpage or other application?

Use the File->Create->Screen Shot menu selection to capture a snapshot of a webpage or application so that you can use the Color Picker on it.

Follow the instructions displayed in the Screen Shot dialog box to capture the contents of any window on your screen.

9.7 Using Color Gradients

Select the Blend Tool from the Toolbox window. Drag your mouse from one side of the image to another. The tool works like Bucket Fill except that it fills with a gradient from the foreground color to the background color.

51

This technique was used to great effect on Harry Squire's *Fade to Black* cover.

9.8   Creating Colored Borders

To create a colored border around a box, simply create two overlaying boxes of slightly different size.

For example, to create a colored border, select a rectangular region (remember, on a new transparent layer) and fill it with your border color. Next, select the inside dimensions of your border and press the Delete key to remove the inside. You should end up with a rectangular box which you can position around image, text, and other colored boxes.

Check out the number of boxes in the cover for Melanie Jackson's "*The Secret Staircase*":

> http://www.melaniejackson.com/images/theSecretStaircase.jpg

9.9   Positioning Text over Colored Boxes

One important use of colored boxes is positioning them behind text so that the text will stand out. For example, white text over a black box can be read quite clearly even in thumbnail.

After creating a rectangular box, position its layer beneath the text layer you'd like to highlight. You might also need to move the text to accommodate available real estate. Remember that you should move text layer contents using the Text Tool and image layer contents using the Move Tool.

One more important point. Try not to obscure important aspects of any images on your cover with your colored boxes.

9.10 Projects

9.10.1 Project 1: Create a Colored Box Cover

Open GIMP, and create a standard-sized book cover with a white background. Use the Select Tools and the Bucket Fill Tool to fill overlaying rectangles with different colors. Each rectangle should be created on its own layer so that it can be moved around individually and overlay other rectangles.

Be sure to use the Rotate Tool to rotate your rectangles into strange angles. Use the Elliptical Select Tool to add some colored circle layers.

What a wild cover, hey? Check out what I managed to accomplish with colored boxes and circles in the *On the Rocks* cover on The Wall of Book Covers.

9.10.2 Project 2: Put a Border around Your Book Cover

If your book cover is white or very pale, you might want to draw a colored box around it to make it stand out when displayed on a white webpage.

Create a 10 pixel-wide colored border around your book. Here's a big hint as to how:

1. As always, the first step is to create a new layer.

2. Choose an appropriate foreground color for your border.

3. Choose the Rectangle Select Tool from the Toolbox window.

4. Drag a rectangular selection in the Image Manipulation window. It doesn't matter what size. You'll be typing in the size in the Rectangle Select Tool parameters section in the lower half of the Toolbox window.

5. Time to type those parameters. The Position of your rectangular selection should be 10 and 10. The Size of your rectangular selection should be your image width (e.g. 1333) - 20 (e.g. 1313) and your image height (e.g. 2000) - 20 (e.g. 1980). Type these numbers into the appropriate selection parameter fields (Position and Size) in the lower half of the Toolbox window.

6. Using the Select->Invert menu selection to invert your selection.

7. Use the Bucket Fill Tool from the Toolbox window to fill your selection with color.

Refer to Lisa Cach's book cover on The Wall of Book Covers.

10 Using Layer Masks

Layer masks represent a powerful aspect of GIMP for producing wild effects. We can't afford to get too wild here, but let's see if we can shake things up a little.

In this chapter we will:

1. Learn what layer masks are.

2. Learn to create, apply, and delete layer masks.

3. Use layer masks to produce various effects using text and images.

10.1 Learning about Layer Masks

A layer mask is a black and white overlay applied to a layer to determine what gets through from beneath. It's like a sieve. Black in a layer mask lets nothing be seen from the associated layer. White allows the contents of the associated layer to be seen. Shades of gray let through phantom shades of the associated layer.

Using a layer mask, you can produce images that fade in and text filled with a color gradient. Actually, there are a lot of applications of layer masks, but these are the two we're about to explore.

10.2 Creating a Layer Mask

As always, begin by ensuring you've selected the layer you want to mask. Right-click on the appropriate layer in the Layers window and select Add Layer Mask from the pop-up menu. The Add Layer Mask dialog box will be displayed. Select either black or white for the layer mask depending if you want nothing or everything in the associated layer to be seen. Click the Add button at the bottom of the dialog box.

The layer mask will appear as a separately selectable box in the Layers window to the right of the associated layer box.

10.3 Using a Layer Mask for Gradient Text

Okay, this is the hardest section in the book. Master this technique and you are king of the world. If you just don't get it, no worries — move on.

1. Create a new transparent layer by clicking on the button at the lower left corner of the Layers window.

2. Create a layer mask by selecting the layer you just created and right-clicking on that layer in the Layers window.

3. Select Add Layer Mask from the pop-up menu. This will display the Add Layer Mask dialog box. Set the layer mask to Black (full transparency) and click the Add button to finish creating the layer mask.

4. Select yellow for your foreground color and red for the background color in the Toolbox window.

5. Insure the layer box and not the layer mask box is selected.

6. Drag a gradient across the Image Manipulation window using the Blend Tool from the Toolbox window.

7. Set the foreground color to white and type some large text into a new text layer in the Image Manipulation window.

8. Use Edit->Copy to copy that new text layer and paste it into the layer mask.

As a result of performing these steps you should see a yellow to red gradient filling your text.

See the *Fade to Black* book cover in the Wall of Book Covers for an extreme example of black to white gradients.

10.4 Using a Layer Mask to Fade In Graphics

1. Select a layer in the Layers window containing graphics you'd like to fade.

2. Add a layer mask to the layer to be effected.

3. Set the foreground color in the Toolbox window to black and the background color to white.

4. Select the Blend Tool from the Toolbox window.

5. Select the layer mask in the Layers window.

6. Drag a gradient across the image in the Image Manipulation window.

As a result of performing these steps you should see a faded ghost version of your image.

10.5 Deleting and Applying a Layer Mask

If you're satisfied with the effect provided by your layer mask (and you're done manipulating the mask), go ahead and apply it to the associated layer by right-clicking on the layer in the Layers window and selecting Apply Layer Mask from the pop-up menu.

If you don't like the effect provided by your layer mask, delete it by right-clicking on the layer in the Layers window and selecting Delete Layer Mask from the pop-up menu.

11 Stroking a Path

Alright, I'm going to leave you with one cool trick for highlighting your text. It's called "Stroking a Path". This trick will produce a line around the text in any text layer. You can use it to make text stand out against a similarly colored image or background.

Follow these steps to produce outlined text.

11.1 Select the Targeted Text Layer

Select the layer in the Layers window containing the text you wish to emphasize. Select the Text Tool in the Toolbox window. Finally, click on the text to be outlined within the Image Manipulation window. A dashed border should appear around the text.

11.2 Generate a Path from Text

Select the "Path from Text" button at the bottom of the Toolbox. This will generate a path which we can use to outline the font.

11.3 Display the Path Window

Select Windows->Dockable Dialogs->Paths to display the Paths window.

11.4 Select the Path

The Paths window may display multiple paths. In this case, select the path you just generated based on its thumbnail by left-clicking the selection.

11.5 Set the Foreground Color

Go to the Toolbox window and select the foreground color box. This is the color that will outline your text, so please choose tastefully. A black outline on white text or a white outline on black text can be striking.

11.6 Select Paint along the Path

Select "Paint along the path" from the icons displayed along the bottom of the Paths window. The Stroke Path window will be displayed.

11.7 Pick the Stroke Width

Change the width of the line to be drawn around the text in the font. The line width is specified in pixels and should be smaller when outlining smaller text sizes and larger when outlining the bigger fonts.

11.8 Stroke the Path

Click the "Stroke" button at the bottom of the Stroke Path window to actually outline your text in the chosen color and width. The results will be displayed in the Image Manipulation window.

Use the Edit->Undo menu option if you don't like the effect. Try again using different outline thicknesses and colors.

Note that this operation will turn a text layer into an image layer.

11.9 Projects

11.9.1 Project 1: Stroking a Path

Create a new book cover using standard dimensions and a white background.

Use the text font Times New Roman at a size of 100 pixels and a color of red to enter the title "Title".

Follow the instruction in this chapter to stroke the path in black using a pixel width of "1".

Use the text font Times New Roman at a size of 300 pixels and a color of blue to enter the title "Title 2" (on a new layer).

Follow the instructions in this chapter to stroke a path in black using a pixel width of "4".

12 Putting It All Together

It's time to apply all the information we've gathered so far into recreating a book cover. Which book cover are we going to recreate? Why the cover to this book, of course. Why? Because it uses only free images, many of the techniques outlined in this book, and you already know what it's supposed to look like.

Without further ado, let us begin....

12.1 Open Gimp

Start GIMP and select the File->New menu option to create a 2000x1333 pixel image.

12.2 Color the Background Layer

You should have only one layer in your image so far, the Background. We're going to color the Background white.

Double-click the foreground image color box around a third of the way down the Toolbox window. Use the color picker to set the foreground color to white and click the OK button at the bottom of the Change Foreground Color window.

Use the Bucket Fill Tool to fill the background with your foreground color (white). Left-click on the Bucket Fill Tool in the Toolbox window then left-click in the body of the Image Manipulation window to fill the background with your new color.

12.3 Color a Rectangular Region

We're now going to make the deep red banner across the upper part of the cover.

Change the foreground color to deep red by double-clicking the foreground color box and entering the color value of "ab0000" in the HTML notation field. Click the OK button at the bottom of the window to complete color selection.

Create a new layer (notice that we do this before creating each new graphical element). Select the new layer. Select the Rectangle Select Tool from the top of the Toolbox window. Drag a rectangular box across the cover at approximately Position 0 by 660 and a Size of 1333 by 550.

Select the Bucket Fill Tool and left-click your mouse within your rectangular selection in the Image Manipulation window to fill the selection with the foreground color.

12.4 Download and Copy the Globe Image

In your browser, go to the following Can Stock Photo URL:

http://www.canstockphoto.com/only-world-globe-1277990.html

Download a free comp of the image by selecting the "comp" link below the image. Pay attention to where you save the image because you're about to open it.

Open the saved image in GIMP using the File->Open menu item.

Use the Image->Canvas Size menu option to resize the globe image to about 800 x 800 pixels.

Drag an Elliptical selection around the image stretching its edges and moving it until it perfectly surrounds the globe. Use the Edit->Copy menu selection to make a copy of the globe.

Add a new transparent layer to your book cover image, above the colored banner, and Edit->Paste the globe over the left hand side of the banner. Use the Move Tool to position the globe on the layer.

12.5 Create and Copy a Logo

Use the File->Create->Logos->SODA Chrome menu item to create the title of your book. This will display the Script-Fu: SOTA Chrome dialog box.

In the dialog box, enter "DO IT YOURSELF:" in the Text box. Enter a Font size 300, a Font of Bondini Condensed.

In the resulting Image Manipulation window, delete the Background layer. Right-click on the other layers and use the Merge Layer Down menu item to merge all the layers into one. Now, use the Rectangle Select Tool to select "DO IT". Edit->Copy the two words.

In your book cover image, create a new layer. Paste and position the "DO IT" text over the top of the cover.

Now, do the same thing to copy the "YOURSELF:" text to its own layer.

12.6 Add Text to the Banner and Body

Now, use the Text Tool from the Toolbox window to type the words "Book" and "Covers" over the red banner. Set the Font to "Imprint MT Shadow", the Size to 250, and the color to white. Use the text tool to move the text into position.

Use the same font with a size of 100 and a color of black to write the text in the body of the book cover.

12.7 Stroke the Author Name

Type the author's name, my name or yours, using the Font Tool in Imprint MT Shadow at a font size of 100 in white.

Notice that the name disappears on the white background. Follow the instructions outlined in the Stroking a Path to stroke the font in black.

12.8 Save Your Work

Use the File->Save As menu selection to save your work as both XCF and JPG files.

13 Final Words

That's it, you're ready to start making book covers.

Before you leave, I'd like to take a moment to go over all the covers in The Wall of Book Covers and explain a little bit about how each one was created.

13.1 Blood Lust

The first cover is the old *Blood Lust* cover. It has a black background layer and half the page is covered by the image of a shirt and tie. The text is simple but I added a couple of graphical teeth on a layer above the text.

The current *Blood Lust* cover is a simple image overlayed by text. The fancy red text I use is called Bleeding Cowboys. I stroked the lettering in black to make it stand out.

13.2 Blood Reich

The next cover is simply two images blended joined in the background with creepy red text overlaying it. Not a lot to say here.

13.3 Book of Dreams

The next four covers are for the Book of Dreams series. The original covers are simple pictures with text over them. A later rendition of *Metropolis* pulls out all the stops using gradient text (layer masks), a stroked font, and a nice box around the image.

13.4 Dead of Night and Demeter

On the *Dead of Night* cover the image fades nicely into the black cover. Notice the use of a layer mask and gradient text that allows a starburst to show through the text lettering.

Demeter uses a black background which nicely blends into the compass image. The text is a created logo using the SODA Chrome font (I deleted the silver layer to expose the gold below).

13.5 Devil Books

The three Devil books are all historical Scottish romances. Notice the attempt to use the font effect to relate them (though *Devil of the Highlands* looks a little too unique). A nice gradient text effect is used. Also, background ghosting is added by severely blurring white lettering.

13.6 Drained

On the *Drained* cover, I cut out the plunger and laid it over a picture of a tombstone. I had to use the Perspective Tool to angle the text into the distance on the tombstone.

13.7 Due North

A nice use of branding, this is the first book in the Butterscotch Jones Mystery Series. With each cover, only the title, color of the blue bar, and bottom image change. All the rest remains the same to brand the books as being common.

13.8 Fade to Black

A nice use of a white to black gradient background with gradient text. Notice that blood stain appears again.

13.9 Rest of the Row

First Son shows the use of the SODA Chrome logo in a fancy font. On the *Fly* cover I used the Rotate Tool to rotate the "Top Sequel" label. Notice on *He's a Magic Man* the use of two different fonts to compose the title. There are five different layers in that title alone. Finally, *In Walked Trouble* shows the power of a simple image and text cover.

13.10 The Kiss

Again, simplicity rules. This cover uses four layers. A black background layer. A layer containing the image that covers the top two thirds of the cover. The title and my name are two separate text layers. That's it.

13.11 Rest of the Row

More cool fonts and images combine to make some nice covers. I used the Free Select Tool to cut out the car and the Egyptian god.

13.12 Moving Violation

One of our original covers which has never been replaced (most of our covers span several versions). The font, slope, and sign are all brands of this series.

13.13 Murder Most Deadly

Is that a cool title effect or what? Yes, I actually cut apart the title text so that I could cant and place each letter in a goofy position. This took time but the effect was well worth it.

13.14 Rest of Row

Of Two Hearts uses a nice reflection technique I created by using the Flip Tool to flip the image vertically. *On the Rocks* shows what can be done with circles and rectangles.

13.15 Portrait of a Gossip

This book uses a 3D cover. These are risky because some sites (e.g. B&N) won't accept them. But they look cool anyway. No, it's not easy to do.

13.16 A Rose by Any Other Name

This cover is surrounded by a colored border. The color was sampled out of the dandelion.

13.17 Sanderson House

Another simple four-layer image. I selected the hand and house off a white background by selecting the white and using Select->Invert. We replaced the original cover because it didn't say "cozy mystery".

13.18 The Rest

More cool images to consider.

Well, that's all for now. Enjoy making book covers on your own, and if you get a chance drop me a line at brianjjaxn@yahoo.com to let me know how you're doing.

14 Conclusion

In the remainder of this series I'll discuss the following self-publishing topics:

Writer's Introduction to the Business of Self-publishing for Beginners

In this book I explain why you should publish your books exclusively on Amazon. I also explain why you should publish a Print on Demand (POD) paperback via KDP.

Creating Book Covers with Microsoft Powerpoint for Self-publishing Beginners

In this book I'll explain how to create a free professional quality book cover using Microsoft PowerPoint 2016. I'll also teach you how to download free cover images from a website called Pixabay and additional book cover creation options including Canva and the GIMP.

Amazon Kindle eBook and POD Paperback Self-publishing for Beginners

In this book I'll explain how to use Microsoft Word 2016 for format your finished manuscript for publication. Formatting will include everything needed for both eBook and POD paperback publication.

I'll also explain how to use the KDP web-based interface to define your Amazon product page and upload your eBook for sale on Amazon. The book then goes on to explain how to perform the similar steps required to publish your book in POD paperback on Amazon.

Amazon Kindle eBook Marketing and Promotion for Self-publishing Beginners

In this book I provide several tips on how to market your book. These marketing tips apply to books on Amazon and assume that you have entered your Amazon eBook into the Kindle Select program. A portion of this book is dedicated to email list marketing using a free MailChimp account.

Fundamental Writing Skills for Self-publishing Beginners

In this book, I explain the fundamentals of writing including words and spaces, punctuation, sentences, paragraphs, dialog and essays.

Questions and comments regarding the contents of this manual should be forwarded to me at brianjjaxn@gmail.com.

Check out all the books in the series at Amazon:

https://www.amazon.com/Brian-Jackson/e/B003SRFYJY/ref=dp_byline_cont_pop_book_1

15 About the Author

Hi, my name is Brian Jackson. I'm the author of over one dozen books. I'm also the publisher of over 100 books. Most of the books I've published were written by my wife, Melanie Jackson. Finally, I'm an instructor with around 50 online training videos published and 125 thousand students on a site named Udemy.

I self-published my first book in the fall of 2014. Later that same year, I convince my wife, who's New York publisher had recently gone out of business, to join me in self-publishing. Together, we ended up earning over half-a-million dollars writing and self-publishing books. During the last seven years I've learned a lot about self-publishing books.

In this book, I will convey some of my hard-won knowledge gained from within the heart of the self-publishing business. It's up to you whether you follow my advice, but it sure can't hurt to read it.

eBooks by Brian Jackson

Remote Control

Travel Logged

Drained

Of Two Hearts

First Son

Blood Lust

Blood Reich

Sanderson House

The First Book of Dreams: Metropolis

The Second Book of Dreams: Meridian

The Third Book of Dreams: Destiny

Dead of Night

The Kiss

In Walked Trouble

Sign-up for My Mailing List

If you haven't already done so, be sure to sign up for my Amazon Kindle eBook Self-publishing for Beginners mailing list so that I can share new insights with you as I continue to hone my craft. Here's what you'll get:

- A free PDF copy of my book *Writer's Introduction to the Business of Self-publishing for Beginners*.
- Receive my weekly email newsletter.
- Receive updates on the *Amazon Kindle eBook Self-publishing for Beginners* series.
- Receive free and discount book offers.
- Receive free and discount Udemy online video training course offers.
- Receive plenty of new advice from the trenches as I continue to stumble upon new information and techniques.

I look forward to continuing to learn with you.

---Brian

www.ingramcontent.com/pod-product-compliance
Lightning Source LLC
Chambersburg PA
CBHW071047220526
45467CB00004B/1703